A Thrill of Hope

A Thrill of Hope

Celebrating Advent at Home

Ashley Wallace

ANGLICAN PASTOR

an imprint of

LEADERWORKS, PLANO, TEXAS

A publication of Anglican Pastor, an imprint of LeaderWorks,
7200 Dallas Parkway, Suite 1022, Plano, TX 75024.

Wallace, Ashley, T., 1974 -.
   A Thrill of Hope: Celebrating Advent at Home
ISBN
Paperback 978-1-7343079-0-0
        Ebook 978-1-7343079-1-7
1. Advent. 2. Advent Traditions. 3. Advent Recipes

Cover Design: John Wallace
Page Design: Blu Design Concepts
Printed in the United States of America

✦ TABLE OF CONTENTS ✦

✴ FOREWORD ✴

AT ANGLICAN PASTOR, we're dedicated to making Anglicanism accessible to everyone from Anglican leaders to the "Angli-curious."

Along those lines, we're convinced that making *Advent* accessible is one of the best possible introductions to the seasons of the Church calendar.

Of course, the Christian year is about more than just changing liturgical colors in a Sunday morning service. The Church calendar is a way of life—a rhythm that's meant to form our families and our friendships.

Now, that sounds good. But how do we live it out on the ground, in our homes?

To answer that question, it really helps to have a good friend as a guide who can speak from experience. That's why we're excited to introduce you to Ashley Wallace and her extremely helpful book, *A Thrill of Hope: Celebrating Advent at Home.*

In the pages that follow, let Ashley be your guide, a source of new ideas (and recipes!) for observing the season of Advent at home with family and friends.

We're convinced that, if you do so, you'll have a lot of fun along the way. But, even more importantly, you'll grow closer to Jesus. Ashley can help you shape your household into a "domestic church" as you prepare for Christmas.

Our King and Savior now draws near: O come, let us adore him! From all of us at Anglican Pastor, we wish you a blessed Advent and a merry Christmas!

Greg Goebel, GENERAL EDITOR
Joshua Steele, MANAGING EDITOR
David Roseberry, PUBLISHER

⋆ PREFACE ⋆

"For everything there is a season" Ecclesiastes 3:1.

Growing up in the south, I didn't know a lot about seasons. I mean, I knew about them from books and movies, but I had never really experienced them. The only seasons we had in the Florida panhandle were kind of hot, hot, and very hot.

When my husband was given the opportunity to attend seminary in Wisconsin, we were nervous to leave our home and family but we were also excited to be making such a radical change and to experience a world filled with seasons that were completely alien to us.

The fall in Wisconsin was beyond anything we could have imagined. Brilliant reds, golds, oranges, and yellows exploded from the trees. Every scene took your breath away, every view looked like a postcard picture. Hooray for seasons! Hooray for us being wild and adventurous! Little did we know, falls in Wisconsin are short-lived and winter comes all too quickly!

In the winter of 2002, I found myself far from the life I once knew. Here I was, a beach girl transplanted to the frosty climes of Wisconsin. For those of you who have never experienced a Wisconsin winter, let me explain: you don't leave the house . . . ever! It is just too cold! Especially when you're from Florida! And seeing as how I had just given birth to my second child; we were housebound in a major way. I felt very isolated and I was left with a lot of time to think. I thought deep thoughts like, "Who am I?" "What is my purpose in the world?" and the much more desperate, "WHAT IN THE WORLD AM I DOING IN WISCONSIN?"

The days were so long and cold. It felt like I did the same thing every day. There seemed to be very little structure to my life and my days felt monotonous and without form. We were Christians so we read Bible stories to our children, we talked to them about Jesus and we sang Christian songs with them but that filled up a very small portion of the day. It just didn't seem like enough to me. I wanted a lot more meaning in my day. I had a deep desire to incorporate the things of God more in my life. I wanted my everyday life to be permeated with the Spirit of the living God.

One night as I was reading a local magazine, I was drawn to an interview with a new chef from a restaurant in nearby Milwaukee. He was describing the foods that he was currently serving. They were all traditional Advent foods from his small village in France. I was so intrigued. I had no idea that other countries, other cultures had particular foods that they made for Advent and Christmas.

A chef who was preparing traditional Advent foods from his village in France? I wondered how many more traditions other cultures have. How many other ways have people celebrated the seasons of the church? I wanted to find out more.

This was an entirely new concept to me that a whole region could be so shaped by the traditions of their faith. I loved it. I started asking a lot of questions and doing a lot of research.

This whole world opened up to me - a world of possibilities. People around the world were living out their faith with traditions that were similar but with regional and ethnic differences based on foods and geographic regions. It reminded me of St. Paul's analogy about the body of Christ in 1 Corinthians. We are all uniquely made and yet we are all one body of Christ.

I began to think about my own little family. Who are we as a family within the larger framework of Christians? What traditions do I want to embrace? I began to get so excited. What if my day could ebb and flow with the greater life of the church? What if my day could be filled with meaning, richness, color, taste . . . things that involve all of our senses? What if I could create an atmosphere of faith in my home, traditions that enriched and gave structure, purpose and unity with the local church and then the wider, worldwide church? Themes of wholeness and identity began to take shape in my heart.

I started researching and collecting traditions from all over the world. I compiled them all and I incorporated these traditions into my own family. During Advent, the

Advent wreath is dressed in evergreen boughs that my children bring in from the woods. We place it on the dining room table and every Sunday we sit down in the darkness, light the Advent candles and learn anew the story of our salvation. As I look around, the light of the candles casts a soft glow and every face is filled with a sense of wonder. This is what celebrating Advent does, it takes the chaos and the frantic rush of our lives and it forces us to slow down. We are given, as a family, time to prepare our hearts for the coming of Christ so that when Christmas finally arrives, we greet the day with true joy.

What you hold in your hand is the result of my personal journey through the seasons of the church. I hope it will bless you as a resource and as a guide through your own journey through the seasons of the church. Here's to embracing all that the seasons of the church have to offer!

Truly, Ashley Wallace

How to Use This Book

Liturgical Color

THE LITURGICAL COLOR is an easy way to incorporate the seasons of the church into our lives. The use of colors to differentiate liturgical seasons became a common practice in the Western church in the fourth century. The colors were created to give a visual cue to everyone in attendance as to what season they were celebrating. The liturgical color for Advent is purple or blue. The purple symbolizes Christ's royalty and our penitence. Blue symbolizes preparation.

Orientation:
What are the Seasons of the Church?
What is Advent?

For those who are new to the liturgical traditions of the Church, we've included a brief introduction to the seasons of the Church calendar, as well as the specific season of Advent.

How to Prepare Our Hearts and Minds for Advent

Because the way our culture gets ready for Christmas is quite different from the way the Church celebrates Advent, we've included some suggestions about how to prepare ourselves, as individuals and as families, for Advent.

Ways to Celebrate Advent

The "Ways to Celebrate" section is included as a starting point for celebrating the Seasons of the Church in your home.

ADVENT TRADITIONS FOR THE ENTIRE SEASON

Some Advent traditions, such as the Advent Calendar and Advent Wreath, last for the entire season. This section contains ideas to celebrate advent that apply to the whole season.

ADVENT TRADITIONS FOR SPECIFIC DAYS

However, some other Advent traditions, such as celebrating the Feast of St. Nicholas (December 6) or the "O Antiphons" (December 17–23), only apply to specific days. Check this section for Advent traditions for particular days.

Remember that none of these Advent ideas are mandates, they are merely ideas given to use or to spark ideas of your own. Be realistic in your selections.

INTRODUCTION

Choose ones that seem interesting and manageable. It is not necessary to do all of them. The ideas are not meant to be a burden or to cause stress. They are meant to be a blessing and to unify you with your friends, family, your church and the church universal as we move through the Seasons of the Church.

Advent Devotions

We have included devotions at the end of each of the special days in this book. It is our hope that these devotions will help to guide you in prayer. They have been designed to be easy to use and understand. Decide on the right time to have a devotion. Right before or after dinner or before bed will often be the best time.

If you have more than one person participating in the devotions, invite different members to be the leader, to read the readings or to light the candles. These devotions need not always be led by one person or with families, by the adults. Also, you may choose to let the Leader read the prayers on behalf of everyone else, or you might prefer to read all of the prayers together.

Read about the upcoming season ahead of time. Make sure that you go over the history or meaning of the season yourself or with your family and explain it in a way that they will be able to understand.

Advent Recipes

Sugar cookies are just the beginning! Although sweets are traditionally off-limits during Advent, there are plenty of special days where culinary delights are allowed and encouraged! This section will teach you how to make everything from Speculatius to Lebkuchen

CHAPTER 1

What are the Seasons of the Church?

THE FAITH OF GOD'S PEOPLE, throughout the history of Israel and the Church, has been a holistic faith. It was a faith that encompassed all areas of the people's lives and that ebbed and flowed with the changing of the seasons. Their faith was individual, but just as important it was a corporate faith. Everyone celebrated the same festivals and rituals together and this gave them a sense of belonging to something bigger than themselves. Theirs was also an experiential faith that involved all of their senses with the use of incense, the eating and abstaining from certain foods, the hearing and teaching of the Word of God, and the singing of spiritual songs.

It was in this way that, for the Jewish people, time became much more than just what the Greeks called *chronos* – the passing of time as a measurable quantity of days and weeks and years. Celebrating the festivals and rituals of their faith sanctified the *chronos* of their lives and made it *kairos*. This is time that is not measured by its duration, but instead by its quality and significance. The festivals and rituals reminded them daily that they had been chosen by God to be His people and that it was their relationship with Him, and nothing else, that gave their lives significance.

When the long-awaited Messiah finally came in the person of Jesus everything changed for those who believed in him. The old festivals told only the first part of the story. Now a new kairos had dawned and new celebrations were necessary.

The creation of the Seasons of the Church, the liturgical calendar that begins each year with the First Sunday of Advent, was the natural and beautiful response to the coming of the Messiah.

He was the fulfillment of Holy Scripture and the consummation of all hopes and desires. The Church experienced Christ's resurrection as the ultimate fulfillment of all things promised by God and so new celebrations were created.

The earliest record we have of what would later develop into the seasons of the Church calendar is the early Church's celebration of Christ's death and resurrection. Saint Irenaeus, who lived during the second century A.D. claimed that the celebration of Christ's death and resurrection went back to the time of Saint Polycarp, a disciple of the Apostle John. This means that the Church, from the very earliest of times, had already begun to celebrate the life of Jesus.

The Church's seasons don't just repeat, they reshape us and reform us, making us more and more like Jesus.

Consequently, an entire liturgical year was created in order to walk the Church, both corporately and individually, through the life and ministry of Jesus. The Church's faith was not something upheld and taught only on Sundays, it was something each member of the Church lived every day. It was an experience.

Through the reading of Scripture, the celebration of the Eucharist, and the observance of the feast days and fast days, we celebrate the major events in the life of Christ and in the life of the Church. We are constantly molded and shaped as we walk through these seasons. In other words, the seasons of the Church are how we are shaped into God's people.

Through the seasons of the Church, we continuously marvel at what God has done for us through His Holy Son, Jesus Christ. He has made a way back to Him, back to abundant life. Because we are so filled with gratitude we want to serve and honor God not just on Sundays but every day with every part of our lives. The Seasons of the Church were created so that our everyday lives would be permeated with the Spirit of the Living God. The Seasons do not take precedence over interior formation but are a means of enrichment.

This book was written to help you move into a deeper, daily walk with God. By incorporating the Seasons of the Church into our lives, we are able to more intentionally honor God with our lives and we are able to move not only individually, but also as a family, as a church and as the church universal through the life and mysteries of Christ.

May you be richly blessed as you embrace this marvelous gift - the Seasons of the Church.

CHAPTER 2

What is Advent?

ALL OF SCRIPTURE is a sacred love story, the love of God the Father for His people. It is a story filled with expectation, longing and fulfillment. From the beginning, God has lovingly walked with us, called to us, searched for us even when we turned from Him over and over again. Throughout the Old Testament, God repeatedly calls his people back to Himself and time and again we remain unfaithful. He sends the prophets to call His people back and with the call to return comes a promise, a promise of hope, a promise of redemption, a promise of restoration, a promise to be made again into the people we were meant to be, a people fully alive in God.

These saving acts of God will be accomplished through a Savior who will come to rescue us and bring us back into fellowship with God. No longer will we strive with God. No longer will we be separated from Him. No longer will we turn from Him because through His Savior, His Messiah, His Anointed one, He will give us new hearts and set us free.

Each Advent, we wait with the prophets and with all of creation for the birth of the promised Savior. The prophets' call grows silent for 400 years and then suddenly, out of nowhere, the Almighty God stretches forth

His hand to a small town and calls a seemingly insignificant young girl and she says, "Yes". The God of the universe humbles himself and makes himself flesh, to fully humble Himself, and to fully walk with us in our sorrow. He takes the form of a helpless babe. It is a great mystery. It is the Incarnation. It is God with us, Emmanuel.

This event is so spectacular, so exceptional, and so important that time itself starts here. The first day of the Church year is the first Sunday of Advent. Advent comes from the Latin "Adventus" and simply means "coming." The Season of Advent begins four Sundays before Christmas and is a time for us to prepare not only for the celebration of the coming of Christ as a babe on Christmas Day, but also for the Second Coming of Christ when He will return in triumph to judge the world.

As mentioned above, the liturgical color for Advent is purple or blue. The purple symbolizes Christ's royalty and our penitence. Blue symbolizes preparation.

In her book, *Around the Year with the Trapp Family*, Maria Von Trapp says that the "whole of Advent is characterized by the boundless desire for the coming of Christ expressed in the liturgy" of the Church. And so we cry out with the Church and with all our hearts:

"Maranatha! Come, Lord Jesus!" And, like creation from Adam until the last prophet, or like Mary expectant with child, we embrace the mystery of waiting and we lovingly prepare our hearts. It is during this time that we look to John the Baptist, the last and

WHAT IS ADVENT?

Just like the Season of Lent is a time to prepare for Easter, the Season of Advent is the time to prepare our hearts for the coming of Christ.

greatest prophet sent by God to prepare us for the Messiah. We turn inward and pray for the Holy Spirit to examine our hearts and our motives and to reveal anything that is unclean within us. We repent of our sins and we strive to offer fruits worthy of repentance.

Advent is also a time to remember those less fortunate than us, those who, like the Holy Family, have very little in this life and no place to rest their weary heads. It is a time to collect alms for the poor and to stretch out our hands in a spirit of charity to bless and to heal those around us. The preparation of Advent is given so that our souls may be restored and so that we might be led, as a Church, into a "more profound delight in His birth." (Maria Von Trapp)

In the world in which we live, we are given no time to prepare for the birth of our Lord and Savior and then no time to celebrate it once we get there.

A Thrill of Hope

Although the Church celebrates the season, Advent is absent from the everyday world in which we live. And sadly, it is also often missing from our own homes. Our entire Christian faith is based upon the birth, death, and resurrection of Jesus. However, Christmas decorations explode into stores right after the Halloween merchandise comes down and then the season abruptly ends the day after Christmas. The very heart of both Advent and Christmas - Jesus - has been ripped away and all we are left with is an abstract "Holiday" season. Songs of Frosty the Snowman and Santa Claus blare over the loudspeaker and we are wished a "Happy Holidays" rather than a "Merry Christmas" by the checkout clerk. The Christmas season has become completely devoid of Christ. For the wider world, it is no better than a hyper-commercialized pagan Holiday. But, let us, as God's people, reclaim the beauty and longing of the season of Advent and celebrate it with the Church throughout the world. Hear these words from the Bidding Prayer which is said each year at the Advent Festival of Lessons and Carols:

> "Beloved in Christ, in this season of Advent, let it be our care and delight to prepare ourselves to hear again the message of the Angels, and in heart and mind to go even unto Bethlehem, to see the Babe lying in a manger.

WHAT IS ADVENT?

Let us read and mark in Holy Scripture the tale of the loving purposes of God from the first days of our disobedience unto the glorious Redemption brought us by his holy Child; and let us look forward to the yearly remembrance of his birth with hymns and songs of praise." *Book of Occasional Services (2004),* p. 31.

CHAPTER 3

How to Prepare Our Hearts and Minds for Advent

ADVENT PROPERLY OBSERVED is radically different from the way most of us celebrate the Christmas season. It is a time of waiting, longing and joy-filled expectations. It is a time to emphasize in every way delayed rather than instant gratification. Advent songs are sung rather than Christmas songs, sweets are off-limits until Christmas, the tree is not decorated until Christmas Eve, and the list goes on and on. All of these things are done intentionally in order to emphasize a spirit of preparation, waiting and longing for the fulfillment of God's promise. Although properly observing Advent can be difficult (especially when the wider world skips it altogether), the feeling of joy when Christmas Eve finally arrives will be that much greater.

Decide personally or as a family how you will mark this time. Make it official by writing your commitments down and hanging them in a prominent place in your home like the refrigerator or on the kitchen wall.

If you have children, allow your children to decorate your commitments with things reminding them of Advent like the Advent color, an Advent wreath, the Holy Family journeying to Bethlehem, sweets with a big

"X" over them (off limits!), or the particular family commitments you have made.

Make sure that you talk to your children about their walk through Advent. Explain to them how you walk through this time as a family will look very different from how the world behaves during this time of the year. Remind them that everything you do during Advent is done in order to prepare our hearts for Jesus. Talk to them about parents who are about to have a baby. They not only open their heart to the child that is yet to be born but they also prepare the child's room, get clothing and blankets ready and pick out a name. We, as God's people are the same way as those parents. We not only prepare for the birth of Jesus in our hearts, but in our actions as well. As God's people, we celebrate Advent to remind ourselves that we are sinners and that we get too caught up in our own wants and desires: what we will eat; what we will wear; what we want to play with, etc.

Make sure that your children understand that God will not be angry with them if they eat a cookie or sing a Christmas carol before Christmas Eve. Advent is something we do for ourselves to help us sanctify the time and remember who we are and what has been done for us by Jesus. It does not help God to love us more, nor will he love us any less. He already loves each of us more than we can imagine.

Ideas for Personal or Family Commitments During Advent

PREPARE TOGETHER.

Commit to preparing your home for Advent. Incorporate the five senses into your home. Put out a candle that reminds you of winter. Create an Advent playlist. Cook some of the Advent recipes found at the back of the book. Add seasonal decor to your home that reminds you of Advent.

EAT TOGETHER.

Decide on the number of times during the week that you will eat together and try to stick to this commitment. When you eat together, pick something to eat that everyone will enjoy so there is no strife at the table! Take your time eating the meal and explain to your children that even though they might be done eating, they will remain at the table to share in the family time.

FAST TOGETHER.

Abstain from the treats that you bake until Christmas Eve, sing Advent songs instead of Christmas carols, wait until Christmas Eve to fully decorate your Christmas tree, watch less television and spend more quality time as a family. Commit to a daily devotion personally or with your family.

PRAY TOGETHER.

Find a time for devotions that best suits your family: at the breakfast table, around the table after dinner, in the children's bedroom right before bed, etc. Give your children roles to play in your time of devotion. Allow them to light the candles, to snuff out the candles, read the scriptures, pray, pick the song that you sing, etc. This is a wonderful way to show your children that they are an important part of God's family and to help them feel included.

SERVE TOGETHER.

Collect alms for the poor. Set up a place for your alms container. Talk to your children about the money they will be collecting. Set an example by adding your money to the container. Talk to them about why we give to the poor. Ask them to identify the poor in your community. Make a point to serve those in need as a family during Advent.

CHAPTER 4

Advent Traditions for the Entire Season

THERE ARE MANY TRADITIONAL ways to observe Advent. All of the following things are given as aids to focus our attention and to mark the passage of Advent. Choose as many as you would like but don't overwhelm yourself or your family with too many. They are given to enrich our lives, not to burden us down. After choosing some, incorporate them into your daily and weekly devotions.

The Advent Calendar

Created in nineteenth-century Germany, Advent calendars are used to mark the days of Advent. For each day of Advent, there is either a window that reveals something when opened or a pouch which might hold one or more of the following: a trinket, piece of candy, a coin, a picture or a Bible verse.

Have your children make their own Advent calendars at home. They can be made to look like a home, church or manger scene with many flaps. Behind each flap have them draw an Advent symbol such as a star, an angel, or another Christian symbol. On the twenty-third of December, all of the flaps are open, but the big entrance flap is still closed. The biggest flap is opened on Christmas Eve and reveals the Holy Child in the manger. Under the Christmas Eve flap, the Advent calendar message traditionally reads: "Today you will know that the Lord is coming to save us and in the morning you will see his glory" (Exodus 16:6-7).

The Advent Wreath

The Advent Wreath is a wreath of evergreens with equidistant candles and a central candle. The wreath is a wonderful visual symbol marking our passage of time through Advent. The Advent Wreath provides a visual focus for your evening family devotions.

The wreath is used as a sign to your family that Christians are joyfully waiting for the coming of our Savior, the Christ Child, as every Sunday in Advent a new candle is lighted. Make an Advent Wreath from a kit or on your own and hang it from the ceiling or place it in the center of your dining table. Gather your family every Sunday night for Evening Prayer, light the appropriate number of candles and pray through your family devotions.

The Advent wreath is full of beautiful symbols. The shape of the circle represents eternity. Evergreens are a traditional Christmas decoration that represent the eternal nature of God. Candles represent a time of preparation and purification as well as the light or presence of Christ. The color of the candles is also symbolic. Violet represents penitence as we prepare our hearts for the birth of our Savior. Blue is also used instead of violet to symbolize a sense of expectancy. The rose or pink candle represents Mary, the willing servant of God and the mother of our Lord. The white candle represents Christ and is lit on Christmas Eve.

THE ORDER EACH CANDLE IS LIT IS ALSO SYMBOLIC.

- The first candle is the Patriarch's Candle and reminds us of the great patriarchs of the Bible who faithfully followed God and who prepared for the coming of the Messiah. On this day, a violet or blue candle is lit.

- The second candle is the Prophet's Candle and reminds us of the great prophets of the Bible who faithfully followed God and called God's people to return to God and to faithfulness. On this day, a violet or blue candle is lit along with the Patriarch's candle.

- The third candle is the Virgin Mary Candle and reminds us of the faithfulness of Mary who responded to God's call to bear the Christ. A rose or pink candle is lit along with the Patriarch's candle and Prophet's candle.

Note: The third Sunday of Advent is often called Gaudete Sunday. Gaudete means rejoice! The opening antiphon for this day is "Rejoice in the Lord always" which in Latin is Gaudete in Domino Semper. On this day the penitent mood lifts and we move into a more joyful time of expectancy as the celebration of Christ's birth draws closer.

- The fourth candle is the John the Baptist Candle. Jesus calls John the greatest of all prophets. He came to proclaim the coming of the Messiah and to prepare the way of the Lord. On this day, a violet or blue candle is lit along with the Patriarch's candle, the Prophet's Candle and the Virgin Mary Candle.

- The fifth and central candle is the Christ Candle and represents the birth of our Savior. Along with the other four candles, the Christ Candle is lit on Christmas Eve, Christmas Day and the subsequent twelve Days of Christmas.

The Great Advent Candle

Traditionally, a lighted candle has always symbolized the presence of Christ. The Great Advent Candle is a tall white candle which is lit every night of Advent. Great Advent candles are notched for every day of Advent and are sold in specialty stores. You can also buy a basic white pillar candle and if you like, you can make marks on the candle for each day of Advent. Burn the candle each night and let it burn to the next notch. Let the Great Advent candle and the Advent wreath be the only light for your family's prayer time. Explain to your children that the candle is the symbol of Jesus, the Light of the World, and is a reminder of the world's spiritual darkness as we wait for the coming of Christ.

Christkindl or The Christ Child Tradition

In many European countries, there is the tradition of the Christkindl. On the first Sunday of Advent, right after evening devotions, the mother of the family appears with a bowl filled with the names of the family members on slips of paper. The bowl is passed around and everyone takes a slip of paper with a name on it. The person whose name one has drawn is now in one's special care throughout Advent. From this day until Christmas, one has to do as many little favors for him or her as one can. One has to provide at least one surprise every single day - but without ever being found out. Maria Von Trapp tells us that this special relationship is called "Christkindl in the old country, where children believe that the Christmas tree and the gifts are brought down by the Christ Child Himself. The person whose name I have drawn and who is under my care becomes for me the little helpless Christ Child in the manger." This creates a wonderful atmosphere of joyful suspense, kindness and thoughtfulness. What a special way to observe Advent as a Family!

The Christmas Crib

It is a powerful anticipation of the mystery of Holy Communion. In many countries, a large wooden crib or manger is placed in the living room on the first Sunday of Advent. The crib is empty and next to it is placed a bag of straw. Every evening, after family prayers, the children in the family come to the crib and place one piece of straw in the crib for every sacrifice or good deed done that day. All of these good deeds and sacrifices are done in order to please the Christ Child. This is an amazing opportunity to encourage your children to prepare for the coming of Christ. You might even make it a tradition to build the manger as a family each year in the days before Advent and then fill it with straw throughout the season.

> *The manger that held baby Jesus is extremely symbolic for Christians. It holds a Eucharistic message: the manger that once held grain for the animals, now holds the very Bread of Life.*

The Christmas Tree

Saint Boniface, an English missionary to Germany in the eighth century, is credited with the creation of the first authentic Christmas tree. He was responsible for firmly establishing the Church in German speaking countries.

When Saint Boniface arrived in Germany, many of the pagan tribes worshiped the trees. In order to show the tribes that the trees themselves had no power, he cut down a tree. He then brought the tree indoors, decorated it with lights and taught the people that they should worship the true God who created the trees. He died a martyr's death and is now widely revered in Germany.

In most parts of the world, the Christmas Tree is not put up until Christmas Eve and is decorated by the parents in secret. When the decorated Christmas tree is revealed to the children, it is with the understanding that the Christ Child decorated the tree.

Note: If waiting until Christmas Eve to decorate the tree will be too hard for your family, why not compromise by putting the tree up on the first day of Advent but decorating it only with Jesse Tree ornaments (see below) and then fully decking the tree on Christmas Eve? Then, after prayerfully moving through Advent, decorating the Christmas tree on Christmas Eve will bring the anticipation of Jesus' birth to a delightful height.

The Jesse Tree

Jesse was the father of the great King David of the Old Testament. In Church art, a design developed showing the relationship of Jesus with Jesse and other biblical figures. This design showed a branched tree growing from a reclining figure of Jesse. The various branches had pictures of other Old and New Testament figures who were ancestors of Jesus. At the top of the tree were figures of Mary and Jesus. This design was often used in stained glass windows in the great medieval cathedrals of Europe.

The use of Jesse Tree ornaments helps us to better understand Jesus as fully human and fully divine and is a way to reclaim Christmas ornaments as sacred.

The modern Jesse tree is an Advent custom using a collection of symbols depicting the biblical story of man's redemption from Adam and Eve to Jesus. The symbolic ornaments of the Jesse tree vary from family to family and can be store bought or homemade. The ornaments are hung on a small tabletop sized tree or on a branch brought in from outside. They can also be used on your Christmas tree. Add one ornament to the Jesse Tree each day, starting on December 1st.

Make your own Jesse Tree ornaments. Paint the symbols onto wooden rounds, carve wood into shapes, embroider them onto linen rounds which are then sewn onto round hoops to hold their shape, paint them on paper, or get your children to use their imagination and make their own!

Advent Music

Advent is the season for Advent songs. Advent songs are very different from the songs of Christmas. Think about "O Come, O Come Emmanuel" and the deep desire for redemption conveyed in the words. The songs of Advent are filled with great longing and expectation. To sing Advent songs rather than Christmas carols will be difficult for most people and contrary to what is being played in secular spaces but focusing on the songs of Advent will only heighten and further emphasize Advent's themes. Not singing Christmas carols throughout Advent will only make them that much more powerful when we finally sing them on Christmas Eve. To make the most of what Advent has to offer musically, attend an Advent Lessons and Carols Service and listen to a good production of Handel's Messiah.

Caroling

Nativity or Christmas Carols were folk songs written and sung by the local community. Saint Francis of Assisi is credited with making Christmas carols an important part of Church services by introducing them during a Christmas Midnight Mass in 1223.

Caroling in the streets and the town square soon became a favorite way to celebrate the joy of Christ's birth. Caroling is one of the oldest customs in Great Britain and goes back to the Middle Ages when beggars, seeking food, money, or drink, would wander the streets singing holiday songs. The traditional period to sing carols is from Saint Thomas's Day (December 21) until Christmas morning.

Christmas Baking

Advent is a wonderful time to bake with children. Baking helps to further emphasize the themes of Advent: preparing gifts for others and waiting until Christmas to enjoy our gifts. Traditionally, most of the Christmas baking is done on Saint Thomas Day (December 21). If any baking is done before then, none of it is eaten (or even tasted) in order to further emphasize the themes of waiting and anticipation in Advent. What a wonderful way to emphasize the joy of the great feast we will celebrate fully on Christmas Day.

Nativity Scene or Crèche

From the very first century of Christianity, pilgrimages were made to the site where Jesus was born in Bethlehem. An altar was built where the manger had been and the Church of the Nativity was built over the sight. Saint Francis of Assisi is credited with the idea of bringing the nativity scene into his hometown.

Saint Francis' nativity scene was created in Greccio, near Assisi on Christmas Eve, in 1223 and used real people and animals. The idea of a nativity scene in one's own town quickly spread throughout Christendom. Shortly thereafter, people began to construct nativity scenes in their own homes. With a home nativity scene, the family slowly adds figures to the scene. On Christmas Eve, the infant Jesus is added to the manger. The wise men are placed far away from the scene and are slowly moved closer but do not arrive at the manger scene until the Feast of the Epiphany on January 6.

Christmas Gifts

In most countries around the world, Christmas gifts are given on Christmas Eve or Christmas Day. However, in some eastern countries, gift giving is reserved for Epiphany in order to celebrate the bringing of gifts by the Magi to the Christ Child.

A major difference between the way the majority of the Christian world and the United States gives gifts has to do with who is believed to give the gifts. In the United States, the historical figure of Saint Nicholas, whose feast day is celebrated on December 6, has largely been replaced by the fictitious character known as Santa Claus. Children are told that Santa Claus is responsible for all (or most) of the gifts on Christmas Day. However, in the rest of the Christian world, children are taught that it is the Christ Child who decorates their Christmas tree and who gives them all of their gifts.

Attributing all gifts to the Christ Child is a wonderful way to demonstrate to your children that "every good and perfect gift" comes from God and the greatest of these gifts is Jesus, sent to save us from our sins and bring us back to God.

Make sure that you teach your children as they grow up that the focus of gift giving should be on what we give rather than on what we receive. We give because God first freely gave to us. He held nothing back! He even gave us his most precious gift - his only Son. Because Jesus became poor, we remember the poor with our gifts. We collect alms for them and buy gifts for them. Everything we do for the poor, Jesus said, we do to him.

Another way to add meaning to gift giving would be to require that every gift your child gives to you be made by their own hands. What if every gift given by your children had been lovingly and thoughtfully handmade? How much more meaningful would they be?

Stockings

The traditional story associated with stockings involves Saint Nicholas. Legend has it that there was a poor man who had three daughters. The man had no money to get his daughters married, and he was worried about what would happen to them after his death. Saint Nicholas was passing through town when he heard the villagers talking about the girls and he wanted to help. He knew that the old man would never accept charity so he decided to help in secret. He waited until it was night and crept into the house with a bag of gold coins for each girl. As he was looking for a place to put three bags, he noticed stockings hung over the mantelpiece for drying. He put one bag in each stocking and left. When the girls and their father woke up the next morning, they found the bags of gold coins and the girls were able to get married. This led to the custom of children hanging stockings or putting out shoes, eagerly awaiting gifts from Saint Nicholas on his feast day, December 6.

★ CHAPTER 5 ★

Advent Traditions for Specific Days

IN ADDITION TO THE OVERALL SEASON of Advent, there are special days to celebrate; feast days where we remember special people in the life of the church and the days of anticipation leading up to Christmas Day

The Eve of Saint Nicholas (December 5)

Saint Nicholas was a real person. He was the Bishop of Myra in the 4th century and took part in the great church council of Nicaea which gave us the Nicene Creed - the one we recite every Sunday in Church! It is said that he was extremely concerned with the welfare of children and there are many legends about his good deeds. (See the story above about Saint Nicholas and the three girls in the section on Christmas Gifts and Stockings.)

Most of the Christian world still remembers Saint Nicholas and celebrates his life on December 6. He is depicted as a bishop of the church, with his cope, mitre, and crozier. When people dress up as Saint Nicholas, they dress like a bishop and when they make cookies

> *Saint Nicholas Day and the eve of his feast are an excellent way to re-educate our children on the true role of Saint Nicholas.*

on his feast day, the cookies are cut out in the shape of a bishop with a staff. But in the United States he has become known as Santa Claus or Jolly old St. Nick and instead remembering him on his feast day, he is believed to give gifts, with the help of elves and flying reindeer, on Christmas morning. He cared for children and for the poor. He gave to people who were in need. He would never have wanted to be the focus of Christmas! Saint Nicholas gave because Jesus had already given everything. Saint Nicholas would point us all back to Jesus.

WAYS TO CELEBRATE

Traditionally, the father of the family dresses as the bishop and visits the family, reminding the children that Christmas is drawing near and urging them to prepare their hearts for the coming of Christ. In South America, children write their letters of request to the Christ Child and it is the bishop, Saint Nicholas who picks them up and delivers them to Jesus.

Make Speculatius (see recipe in the recipe section), a traditional cookie made in the Rhineland. It is a gingerbread cookie, specially made for Saint Nicholas Day. It is in the shape of a bishop with a staff.

Have your children put out their Christmas stockings on this night. Fill them while they are asleep with candies and cookies.

The Feast of Saint Nicholas (December 6)

WAYS TO CELEBRATE

When the children discover their filled stockings on Saint Nicholas Day, tell them the story of Saint Nicholas and the three girls. Explain to them that our stockings are filled today to remind us of the way that Saint Nicholas blessed those in need. Today we are called to remember those in need too.

It is traditional in Germany to make Lebkuchen or German honey cakes on this day. A Dutch tradition is to make Bisschopswijn or Bishop's Wine which is a Spiced wine. It is also traditional to make more Speculatius cookies on this day. Recipes for each of these items can be found at the end of this book.

The Last Days Before Christmas

All of the great feasts of the Church year (Christmas, Epiphany, Easter and Pentecost) are followed by times of great merrymaking. It is not enough to celebrate only on the feast day itself, many days of feasting and merrymaking are given to fully celebrate the magnitude of the day. Christmas, however, is the only feast day that is also preceded by a time of merrymaking known in some countries as an octave (eight days) or a novena (nine days).

The time before Christmas serves to increase our already growing sense of eagerness and expectation for the Christ to come.

Seeking Shelter, La Posada, Golden Nights (December 16–24)

We are now moving into the last days before the birth of Christ, only nine days away, and so a remarkable build-up of traditions begin. December 16 is the night when an ancient custom is celebrated all over the world which is known by many different names; La Posada (The Inn) in Spanish-speaking countries, Golden Nights in Central Europe, Seeking Shelter in Austria. The events in the journey of Mary and Joseph from Nazareth to Bethlehem are commemorated at this time.

Nine families from a local parish are chosen to participate in this event. Each family that participates acts as the innkeepers. Neighborhood children and adults act as the pilgrims, who request lodging by going from house to house singing a traditional song requesting shelter for poor Mary and Joseph. The pilgrims carry small lit candles in their hands, and people carry small statues of Joseph leading a donkey, on which Mary is riding. At each house, the "innkeepers" respond to the song by refusing lodging (also in song). Finally, on Christmas Eve, the weary travelers reach the final home, where Mary and Joseph are finally recognized and allowed to enter. In this last home where Mary and Joseph are finally received, candles are lit and everything is lovingly prepared.

The procession enters the home and everyone kneels around the Nativity scene to pray. A large cradle is waiting and a statue of the infant Jesus is placed on a bed of straw and gently rocked while everyone sings a traditional lullaby. In Latin American countries most people sing the beautiful A La Rurru Niño - Babe in Arms. At the end of the long journey, everyone joins together for Christmas carols, feasting, firecrackers, and noisemakers.

In South America, children begin to write letters to the Christ child, telling of their hopes for Christmas. Saint Nicholas picks the letters up and delivers them to baby Jesus. The letters are written from December 16-24 and are left next to the manger in the family's Nativity Scene.

WAYS TO CELEBRATE

Before your evening devotion, assemble the family and sing advent songs as you process the creche figures of Mary, Joseph and the don- key into the living room. Put the figures in a special place of honor and light a candle next to them. Remind your children that we are trying to create an atmosphere of consideration and unselfishness for Mary and Joseph.

A variation of this is to allow each of your children to make up for the harsh treatment that the holy couple received by hosting the figures in their room for the day. Instead of processing the figures into the living room, process them to the door of the first child's room while singing Advent songs. Explain to your children that when it is their turn, they should do everything possible to create a warm and loving atmosphere for Mary and Joseph. Suggest cleaning their room, clearing a spot on their dresser for the figures, placing fresh evergreens around the figures, or ribbons, etc.

Have your children write letters to baby Jesus, expressing their wishes for Christmas. This is a great way to re-educate your children, helping them to see that their Christmas gifts are from God, the giver of all good gifts.

O Antiphons (December 17–23)

The "O Antiphons" are another tradition which begins the final countdown to Christmas Day. The "O Antiphons" are brief scripturally based prayers focusing on the titles given to Christ by the prophet Isaiah. The Antiphons are traditionally prayed before and after Mary's Song, the Magnificat, during Evening Prayer. One antiphon is prayed each evening, from December 17 until December 23. The Octave is completed by repeating all of the Antiphons on December 24.

During these last days, our prayers and our expectations

arise with an ever increasing crescendo. O Come, O Come Emmanuel is one of the Church's oldest and best loved hymns and is based on the O Antiphons. Each stanza begins with one of the names for Jesus found in the Antiphons. It was meant to be sung during this octave with a new verse added each day.

Christians around the world are so eager for the birth of Christ, that we cry out with one voice for Christ to come - and come quickly!

WAYS TO CELEBRATE
- Add the Antiphons to your daily devotion.

- Sing O Come, O Come Emmanuel during your evening devotion.

- Show your children how each O Antiphon is used in the song.

- Listen to the O Antiphons in Gregorian chant. (You can google them and easily find them on YouTube!)

- Write the O Antiphons out as a family and set them out to be read together as part of your evening devotion.

Here are the O Antiphons:

DECEMBER 17 - O SAPIENTIA

O Wisdom, coming forth from the mouth
of the Most High,
reaching from one end to the other mightily,
and sweetly ordering all things:
Come and teach us the way of prudence.
cf Ecclesiasticus 24.3; Wisdom 8.1

DECEMBER 18 – O ADONAI

O Adonai, and leader of the House of Israel,
who appeared to Moses in the fire of the burning bush
and gave him the law on Sinai:
Come and redeem us with an outstretched arm.
cf Exodus 3.2; 24.12

DECEMBER 19 - O RADIX JESSE

O Root of Jesse, standing as a sign among the
peoples;
before you kings will shut their mouths,
to you the nations will make their prayer:
Come and deliver us and delay no longer.
cf Isaiah 11.10; 45.14; 52.15; Romans 15.12

DECEMBER 20 - O CLAVIS DAVID

O Key of David and sceptre of the House of Israel;
you open and no one can shut; you shut and no
one can open:

Come and lead the prisoners from the prison house,
those who dwell in darkness and the shadow of death.
cf Isaiah 22.22; 42.7

DECEMBER 21 - O ORIENS

O Morning Star,
splendour of light eternal and sun of righteousness:
Come and enlighten those who dwell in darkness
and the shadow of death.
cf Malachi 4.2

DECEMBER 22 - O REX GENTIUM

O King of the nations, and their desire,
the cornerstone making both one:
Come and save the human race,
which you fashioned from clay.
cf Isaiah 28.16; Ephesians 2.14
December 23 - O Emmanuel
O Emmanuel, our King and our lawgiver,
the hope of the nations and their Saviour:
Come and save us, O Lord our God.
cf Isaiah 7.14

Feast of Saint Thomas (December 21)

Saint Thomas was one of Jesus' twelve apostles and is
best known for not believing that Jesus had been raised
from the dead when the other apostles told him they had

seen Jesus alive. He is thought to be the only Apostle who went outside the Roman Empire to preach the Gospel. He is also believed to have crossed the largest area, including the Persian Empire and India. He was martyred for leading an Indian Queen to faith in Jesus.

WAYS TO CELEBRATE

The Feast of Saint Thomas is the traditional day to begin all of your Christmas baking. From now on, the house will be filled with delicious smells as you bake for Christmas. Include your children in as much of the baking as possible. Remember that the baking that you do further emphasizes the Advent themes of preparation and of waiting. During this time, cook your choicest delicacies and favorite treats. In many countries, particular cookies are made only for Christmas. The cookies keep for a long time and are often hung on the Christmas tree. What a wonderful way to emphasize the significance of the season with what we cook!

Throughout Austria, this is the day in which Kletzenbrot is baked. Kletzenbrot is a delicious bread with dried fruit in it. One large loaf is made for the family to eat on Christmas morning and then small loaves are made for every member of the family. In Germany, they make a bread called Cristollen which is folded up to look like Christ's diapers. (See recipes in the recipe section below.)

Christmas cookies are also traditional during this time. Each country has its own particular kind. United

States and Great Britain make sugar cookies and Germany makes a sugar cookie called Springerles and a cookie called Lebkuchen, which means Bread of Life. During this time, Gingerbread cookies and Gingerbread houses are also traditional.

Christians throughout the world use December 21-23 to prepare for the Christmas feast. Every plate is piled high with cookies and treats. Although there are sweets all around, it is best to abstain from these sweets until Christmas. No one is even allowed to taste them. This all serves to increase the sense of anticipation and excitement leading up to Christmas.

With all of the baking and preparation, the children begin to see that the birth of Jesus is almost here!

They will hardly be able to wait! This is an excellent opportunity to teach your children delayed gratification and to increase their desire for Christmas to arrive. And remember, the cookies and treats will taste that much better because everyone waited for them. By midnight on December 23, all baking should be completed and everything should be stored away.

Christmas Eve (December 24)

The liturgical color is white or gold which symbolizes a high, holy day

A Thrill of Hope

On Christmas Eve, we are suspended between two worlds - the world of darkness, sin and death and the new world of light promised through God's Messiah. On this day, the season of Advent draws to an end and the waiting and intentional preparation comes to a close. Christmas Eve is our last opportunity to heed the words of Saint John the Baptist and to "prepare the way of the Lord". That is why, traditionally, Christmas Eve is a day for confession. Although we seek on this day to continue to prepare our hearts through confession and introspection, it is hard to contain our excitement be- cause we know what happens at the stroke of midnight - the dawn of a new age, the birth of a Savior who will ransom us from sin and death and bring us back to God!

WAYS TO CELEBRATE

On the morning of December 24, most of the preparations for Christmas Day have been completed. All cookies and treats have been hidden away. The kitchen should look sober and bare compared to the night before with nothing left out but the makings of a very frugal breakfast and lunch. Traditionally, Christmas Eve is one of the strictest fast days of the Christian year. All over the world, many people consume no more than a cup of coffee and a piece of bread for breakfast and lunch is usually water and a small meat-less meal. With these frugal meals, the holy season of Advent draws to a close.

Remember that Christmas Day is one of the highest feast days of the Christian year. We celebrate the birth of our Savior, Jesus. Christmas is what all of Advent has been getting us ready for.

Christmas Eve should be a day of great anticipation and preparation.

It is a wonderful opportunity to provide a sense of wonder and joy for your family that is focused on the birth of the Christ Child. Make this a very special family day where everyone stays home so that you can all watch, wait and prepare together. Allow and encourage your children to participate in all of these activities in order to create a sense of excitement. Christmas Eve is the final day of preparation for the Christmas Feast. Use this day as a time to prepare not only your home, food and clothes, but also to prepare your heart for the joy to come.

CLEAN HOUSE!
As a final act of preparation, it is an Irish and Eastern European tradition to clean your house, return all borrowed items, and fix everything in your house that needs to be repaired. Read the final Advent calendar message: "Today you will know that the Lord is coming to save us and in the morning you will see his Glory!"

A Thrill of Hope

HANG THE FINAL JESSE TREE ORNAMENT AND/
OR DECORATE YOUR CHRISTMAS TREE

Traditionally, in most parts of the world, the Christmas Tree is not put up until Christmas Eve. And when it is put up, it is oftentimes decorated by the parents in secret. When the decorated Christmas tree is revealed to the children, it is with the understanding that the Christ Child has blessed them with both the gifts and the decorations.

When the children wake up on Christmas Eve morning, have the door to the living room closed or curtained off. This will be the room where the tree and presents are put. Having the room closed off creates a sense of mystery and excitement for the children. Tell your children that no one is allowed to go in that room all day because this is where the Christ Child will bless them with gifts and a fully decorated tree. Post a sign on the door that says, "Please, Keep Out".

In the afternoon, send your children to their rooms for a time of quiet. Lay out special books on each of their pillows. Use Advent and Christmas books collected and saved until this time so that they are special and entertaining. They can also be taken by a loved one or relative to play outside or visit relatives. While the children are occupied, go into the room and prepare it for Christmas Eve. This is a great time for the parents to quietly reflect on the birth of Christ, to relax and to enjoy what this day means. Turn on Handel's Messiah while you work. Bring in the Christmas tree and fully decorate it. Refresh the

Advent wreath and place the presents under the tree. Decorate the dining table and set it for a Christmas feast. Set out all of the cookies and foods you have prepared in advance. Place the Christmas crib by the tree. Place a bell next to the Nativity scene.

SERVE A CHRISTMAS EVE MEAL

The Christmas Eve meal is really the very last moment of Advent. It is one of the two or three most important meals of the Christian year and is lovingly referred to as the "Holy Meal". It is a time where Christian families reaffirm their bonds of love and solidarity. Like Christmas Eve itself, the Christmas Eve meal, while still preparing us, is full of a joyful expectancy and is very celebratory in its nature. To reflect this, the Christmas Eve meal is a type of fast within a feast.

It's a jubilant abstinence! Meat is traditionally abstained from during this meal. Each country has its own beautiful food traditions for this night mostly centering around a fish dish and lavish desserts. Every detail of the meal is rich with meaning. For instance, in many countries, the meal begins when the first star appears in the sky reminding us of the star of Bethlehem. The meal is candlelit with a large white candle in the center of the table symbolizing Christ as the Light of the World. Next to the candle is a round loaf of bread symbolizing Christ as the Bread of Life. Also, there are either twelve courses or twelve desserts served to represent the twelve disciples.

In Slavic countries, the floor and dining table are strewn with straw in honor of the stable and a white tablecloth representing the swaddling clothes that the infant Jesus was wrapped in is placed over the dining table's straw. The father breaks thin wafers with religious motifs known as the bread of angels and distributes a piece to each member of the family. As the father distributes the wafer pieces, he kisses each member of his family and wishes them a blessed Christmas.

> **The Christmas Eve meal is a beautiful symbol of love and unity in Christ.**

An extra place is always set at the table in honor of those who are absent. Traditionally, all members of the household sit down and eat together, including servants.

ATTEND THE CHRISTMAS EVE SERVICE
AT YOUR CHURCH.
If attending the service is not possible, after the Christmas Eve meal, Gather the family around the Advent wreath one last time conduct an evening devotion.

The Feast of the Nativity (Christmas Day: December 25)

The liturgical color is white or gold which means a high, holy day.

Joy to the World! The Lord has come!
Let earth Receive her King!

The birth of our long-awaited Savior has finally come!

Christmas Day is a feast day of the highest order.

It is the day of days which celebrates the mystery of the Incarnation. The God of the universe humbled himself, took on flesh and walked among us. Finally we are able to celebrate with Christians all over the world the long-awaited birth of Christ!

As we celebrate, we remember with joy the message of the angels, "Glory to God in the highest, and on earth peace, good will towards men" (Luke 2:14). It is with these words that we see clearly the loving hand of God. God has sent to us a Savior, his very son, Jesus, to redeem us, to set us free, and to bring us back to himself. What a glorious day this is!

Ways to Celebrate Christmas
IDEAS FOR FAMILY COMMITMENTS DURING CHRISTMASTIDE

- It is traditional to greet each other with a kiss and the words: "Christ is Born!," to which the one being greeted responds: "Glorify Him!"

• Attend Christmas Day services at your church or have a family devotion.

• Remember that the bulk of the cooking should have been done by today so that Church can be attended and the immensity of the day be relished and enjoyed.

• Sing Christmas carols! This is the time to sing them to yourself and with your family. Go over the words - really think about what they say and what they mean in your life.

• This is also a day to remember and include the lonely and those who have recently lost loved ones.

• If you have a nativity scene, start moving the three kings (placed some distance away) closer to the manger. Time the movement of the kings to last until the Feast of the Epiphany on January 6.

CHRISTMAS DAY MEAL
This is the day for the festive and extravagant Christmas feast. Christmas Day is also the time to serve the Christmas plum pudding.

To serve the Christmas pudding, the lights are turned out and warmed brandy or rum is poured over the pudding and set ablaze.

The Christmas feast is the time to serve your choicest delicacies in order to celebrate the birth of our Savior.

The flaming pudding is brought to the dinner table to be served as soon as the flame burns out. The pudding is filled with all of the good things of this world to remind us of Christ who will bring with Him on His birthday all the good things of heaven. After the meal, the family gathers in the Christmas room for a family devotion and the singing of carols. During this time in the Christmas room, serve something warm to drink like the French version of hot chocolate or spiced cider.

CHRISTMAS SYMBOLS

The Christmas season is full of many rich symbols. Green and red are the traditional colors which represent the blood of Christ and the eternal life bought for us through Christ. Holly, a traditional Christmas plant, represents the crown of thorns. The Poinsettia, with its star-like petals represents the Star of Bethlehem. Rosemary has always been associated with Christmas because tradition has it that it was the bush used by Mary to dry baby Jesus' clothes.

CHAPTER 6

Advent Devotions

INSTRUCTIONS FOR THE DEVOTIONS: Because the first Sunday of Advent is always four Sundays before Christmas, the date of the first Sunday of Advent changes each year. We have provided readings for each day of Advent, but on some years there will be fewer days than readings. You may wish to incorporate more readings as Christmas approaches so that you can experience all of the readings for Advent.

Each week of Advent has its own devotional with readings for each day of the week.

- On the first Sunday of Advent and each day of that week, use the devotional for the first Sunday of Advent.

- On the second Sunday of Advent and each day of that week, use the devotional for the second Sunday of Advent, and so on.

FIRST DAY OF ADVENT, FIRST SUNDAY OF ADVENT
If a Great Advent Candle is being used it should be
lit at this time or the first candle in your Advent Wreath.
Begin your devotion time with the following invitation to prayer:

Leader: The Lord be with you.
People: And also with you.
Leader: Let us pray.

A Thrill of Hope

Opening prayer:
God of Abraham and Sarah, and all the patriarchs of old, you are our Father too. Your love is revealed to us in Jesus Christ, Son of God and Son of David. Help us in preparing to celebrate his birth to make our hearts ready for your Holy Spirit to make his home among us. We ask this through Jesus Christ, the light who is coming into the world. Amen.

The Patriarch Candle (the first violet or blue candle) is lit on the Advent Wreath at this time.

Read: Creation - Genesis 1-2:3

Use this time for other Advent observances: adding hay to the Christmas Crib, hanging a new Jesse Tree ornament, or adding figures to the Nativity Scene.

Close with a prayer thanking God for his goodness and asking for his guidance and protection for you and all who are in any need or trouble. End your devotion by saying the Lord's Prayer together.

SECOND DAY OF ADVENT
Adam and Eve
Genesis 2

THIRD DAY OF ADVENT
The Fall
Genesis 3

FOURTH DAY OF ADVENT
Noah and the Ark
Genesis 6:12-7:24

ADVENT DEVOTIONS

FIFTH DAY OF ADVENT
Noah and the Flood
Genesis 8-9

SIXTH DAY OF ADVENT
Call of Abraham
Genesis 12:1-9,15:1-5

SEVENTH DAY OF ADVENT
Birth of Isaac
Genesis 21:1-6

EIGHTH DAY OF ADVENT, SECOND SUNDAY OF ADVENT
If a Great Advent Candle is being used it should be lit at this time.
Begin your devotion time with the following invitation to prayer:

Leader: The Lord be with you.
People: And also with you.
Leader: Let us pray.

Opening prayer:
God our Father, you spoke to the prophets of old of a Saviour
who would bring peace. You helped them to spread the joyful
message of his coming kingdom. Help us, as we prepare to celebrate his birth, to share with those around us the good news of
your power and love. We ask this through Jesus Christ, the light
who is coming into the world. Amen.

The Patriarch and the Prophet Candles (the first and second violet or blue
candles) are lit on the Advent Wreath at this time.

Read: Jacob and Esau - Genesis 27

A Thrill of Hope

Use this time for other Advent observances: adding hay to the Christmas Crib, hanging a new Jesse Tree ornament, or adding figures to the Nativity Scene.

Close with a prayer thanking God for his goodness and asking for his guidance and protection for you and all who are in any need or trouble. End your devotion by saying the Lord's Prayer together.

NINTH DAY OF ADVENT
Joseph
Genesis 37

TENTH DAY OF ADVENT
Moses
Exodus 6:1-13

ELEVENTH DAY OF ADVENT
The Red Sea
Exodus 14:5-31

TWELFTH DAY OF ADVENT
Manna from Heaven
Exodus 16

THIRTEENTH DAY OF ADVENT
Joshua, The Warrior Leader
Joshua 1

FOURTEENTH DAY OF ADVENT
David Chosen to be King
1 Samuel 16:1-13

ADVENT DEVOTIONS

FIFTEENTH DAY OF ADVENT, THIRD SUNDAY OF ADVENT
If a Great Advent Candle is being used it should be lit at this time.
Begin your devotion time with the following invitation to prayer:

Leader: The Lord be with you.
People: And also with you.
Leader: Let us pray.

Opening prayer:
God our Father, the angel Gabriel told the Virgin Mary that she was to be the mother of your Son. Though Mary was afraid, she responded to your call with joy. Help us, whom you call to serve you, to share like her in your great work of bringing to our world your love and healing. We ask this through Jesus Christ, the light who is coming into the world. Amen.

The Patriarch and Prophet Candles (the first and second violet or blue candles) are lit on the Advent Wreath followed by the Mary Candle (the rose or pink candle).
Read: David and Goliath - I Samuel 17

Use this time for other Advent observances: adding hay to the Christmas Crib, hanging a new Jesse Tree ornament, or adding figures to the Nativity Scene.

Close with a prayer thanking God for his goodness and asking for his guidance and protection for you and all who are in any need or trouble. End your devotion by saying the Lord's Prayer together.

SIXTEENTH DAY OF ADVENT
The Good Shepherd
Psalm 23

SEVENTEENTH DAY OF ADVENT
Naaman and the Girl
2 Kings 5

EIGHTEENTH DAY OF ADVENT
Messianic Prophecies
Isaiah 9:1-7 and 11

NINETEENTH DAY OF ADVENT
Daniel and the Lion's Den
Daniel 6

Twentieth Day of Advent
Jonah and the Whale
Jonah 1-3
TWENTY-FIRST DAY OF ADVENT
The People are Reunited with God's Law but Then They Rebel
Nehemiah 8:1-12, Malachi 3

TWENTY-SECOND DAY OF ADVENT,
FOURTH SUNDAY OF ADVENT
If a Great Advent Candle is being used it should be lit at this time.
Begin your devotion time with the following invitation to prayer:

Leader: The Lord be with you.
People: And also with you.
Leader: Let us pray.

Opening prayer:
God our Father, you gave to Zechariah and Elizabeth in their old age a son called John. He grew up strong in spirit, pre-pared the people for the coming of the Lord, and baptized

them in the Jordan to wash away their sins. Help us, who have been baptized into Christ, to be ready to welcome him into our hearts, and to grow strong in faith by the power of the Spirit. We ask this through Jesus Christ, the light who is coming into the world. Amen.

The Patriarch, Prophet, and Mary Candles are lit on the Advent Wreath followed by the John the Baptist Candle (the final violet or blue candle).

Read: The Birth of Jesus Foretold - Luke 1:26-38

Use this time for other Advent observances: adding hay to the Christmas Crib, hanging a new Jesse Tree ornament, or adding figures to the Nativity Scene.

Close with a prayer thanking God for his goodness and asking for his guidance and protection for you and all who are in any need or trouble. End your devotion by saying the Lord's Prayer together.

TWENTY-THIRD DAY OF ADVENT
Mary and Elizabeth
Luke 1:39-56

TWENTY-FOURTH DAY OF ADVENT, CHRISTMAS EVE
FAMILY DEVOTION FOR CHRISTMAS EVE
If a Great Advent Candle is being used it should be lit at this time. All of the outer candles on the Advent Wreath should also be lit.
Begin your devotion time with the following invitation to prayer:

Leader: The Lord be with you.
People: And also with you.
Leader: Let us pray.

A Thrill of Hope

Opening prayer:
Lord Jesus Christ, on this day we celebrate your birth at Bethlehem and we are drawn to kneel in wonder at heaven touching earth: accept our heartfelt praise as we worship you, our Savior and our eternal God. Amen.

The Christ Candle in the center of the Advent Wreath should be lit at this time.

Read Luke 2:1-20
After the reading, sit in silence with your family and contemplate the mystery of the Incarnation - God taking on our flesh in the person of his Son, Jesus.

Close with a prayer thanking God for his goodness and asking for his guidance and protection for you and all who are in any need or trouble. End your devotion by saying the Lord's Prayer together and singing an Advent hymn.

While the family is singing, have the mother or father quietly slip into the living room, open the door or curtain and ring the bell by the manger.

Traditionally it is understood that it is the Christ Child who rings the bell announcing what He has done for the family. When the bell is heard, blow out the Advent candles and head for the living room. We are now moving from Advent into Christmas!

CHAPTER 7

Advent Recipes

Plum Pudding

Traditionally made on Stir-Up Sunday or the First
Sunday in Advent and served on Christmas Day

⅔ cup each:

currants

dark raisins

golden raisins

dates or prunes, chopped

¾ cup chopped candied orange or lemon peel

½ cup brandy, rum, sherry or cider

1 cup fine breadcrumbs

1 teaspoon cinnamon

½ teaspoon ground ginger

¼ teaspoon nutmeg

¼ teaspoon ground cloves

1 teaspoon salt

1 ½ cups dark or light brown sugar

1 ½ cups stout, ale, beer or milk

4 eggs, well beaten

⅔ cup beef suet, finely chopped

¾ cup flour

1 ½ teaspoons baking powder

½ teaspoon baking soda

Freshly grated rind of one lemon
Freshly grated rind of one orange
½ cup finely chopped blanched almonds
⅔ cup peeled, cored, chopped apples

Combine the dried and candied fruits. Pour the brandy over them and let them sit for at least 1 hour. Mix the crumbs with the spices, salt and brown sugar. Pour the stout over them and let stand for a few minutes. Blend the eggs with the suet. Sift the flour with the baking powder and baking soda. Combine all these mixtures and add the remaining ingredients: the rinds, the almonds and the apples. Turn this mixture into a well-buttered and sugared 2-quart mold. Cover well with aluminum foil. Place the mold on a rack in a large pan. Pour in 2 to 3 inches of water. Cover the pot well. Steam for about three hours, or until the pudding is firm. (A knife inserted into the middle of the pudding should come out clean. You will need to unwrap the pudding to check and then re-wrap.) Store in the refrigerator; to re-heat, steam for an hour or so. From A Continual Feast

Speculatius

Made for the Eve and the Feast of Saint Nicholas and the baking days for Christmas.

1 cup butter
1 cup shortening

2 cups brown sugar
1/2 cup sour cream
1/2 teaspoon soda
4 teaspoons cinnamon
1/2 teaspoon nutmeg
1/2 teaspoon cloves
4.5 cups sifted flour
1/2 cup chopped nuts

Cream the butter, shortening and sugar. Add sour cream alternately with sifted dry ingredients. Stir in nuts. Knead the dough and shape into rolls. Wrap the rolls in plastic wrap and chill overnight. Roll the dough very thin and cut into shapes. Bake at 350 degrees for 10 to 15 minutes.

Bisschopswijn or Bishop's Wine

Traditionally made for the Eve of the Feast of Saint Nicholas

2 bottles full -bodied red wine
1 orange, studded with cloves and quartered
1 strip lemon peel
1 stick of cinnamon
1/4 teaspoon each: mace, allspice, ground ginger
2 to 4 tablespoons sugar to taste

Pour the wine into a saucepan. Add the orange, lemon peel, stick of cinnamon and spices. Simmer for 5 to 10 minutes. Add sugar to taste. Serve hot.

Kletzenbrot (Bread with Dried Fruit)

Made on the Feast of Saint Thomas

2 cups whole wheat flour
1 cup white flour
2/3 cup brown sugar
3 tsp. baking powder
2 tsp. baking soda
1/4 tsp. salt
2 cups buttermilk
1 cup chopped nuts
1 cup chopped prunes
1 cup chopped figs
1 cup chopped dates
1/2 cup raisins
1/2 cup currants

Mix sifted dry ingredients in a bowl. Add buttermilk slowly and stir to a smooth dough. Mix in the nuts, raisins, and the rest. Bake in a hot oven for about an hour.

Cristollen

Made on the baking days before Christmas and Christmas Eve

4.75 to 5.25 cups all-purpose flour
2 packages active dry yeast

1 teaspoon ground cardamom

1.25 cups milk

1/2 cup sugar

1/2 cup butter

3/4 teaspoon salt

1 egg

1 cup diced mixed candied fruits and peels

1 cup raisins

3/4 cup chopped walnuts

1 tablespoon finely shredded lemon peel

In a large mixing bowl stir together 2 cups of flour, yeast, and cardamom. In a medium saucepan heat and stir the milk, sugar, butter, and salt until warm (120-130 degrees) and butter is almost melted. Add to flour mixture along with egg. Beat with an electric mixer on low speed for 30 seconds, scraping bowl constantly. Beat on high speed for 3 minutes. Using a spoon, stir in candied fruits and peels, raisins, walnuts, and lemon peel; stir in as much of the remaining flour as you can.

Turn out onto a lightly floured surface. Knead in enough remaining flour to make a moderately soft dough that is smooth and elastic (3 to 5 minutes total). Shape into a ball. Place in a greased bowl; turn once to grease surface. Cover and let rise in a warm place until double (about 1 to 1.5 hours).

Punch dough down. Turn out onto a lightly floured surface. Divide dough in half; divide each half into thirds.

Cover and let rest for 10 minutes. Meanwhile, grease 2 baking sheets.

With hands, roll each piece of dough into a 1-inch-thick rope about 15 inches long. Line up 3 of the ropes, 1 inch apart, on prepared baking sheet. Starting in the middle, loosely braid by bringing the left rope under the center rope. Repeat to end of loaf. On the other end, braid by bringing alternate ropes over center rope from center. Press rope ends on each side together to seal. Repeat braiding with the remaining 3 ropes on other prepared baking sheet. Cover and let rise until nearly double (about 1 hour).

Brush loaves with milk. Bake in a 350-degree oven for 20 to 25 minutes or until golden and loaves sound hollow when tapped. (Switch baking sheets to a different oven rack halfway through baking time to ensure even baking.) If necessary, cover with foil the last few minutes to prevent over browning. Remove from baking sheets.

Cool on wire racks.
Makes 32 servings.

Sugar Cookies

Made on the baking days before Christmas

1 cup butter
1.5 cups sifted confectioner's sugar
1 egg
1 teaspoon vanilla
1/2 teaspoon almond
2.5 cups flour
1 teaspoon soda
1 teaspoon cream of tartar

Cream the butter and sugar. Add the egg and extracts. Sift flour, soda, and cream of tartar together. Add to butter mixture. Wrap dough in plastic wrap and chill overnight. Roll out and cut into desired shapes. Bake in a 350-degree oven for 10 to 12 minutes.

Icing is simply confectioner's sugar mixed with teaspoons of half and half until desired consistency is reached. To color the icing, add food coloring of choice.

Lebkuchen (A German Honey Cake)

Made on the Feast of Saint Nicolas and on baking days before Christmas

1 & 1/3 cups honey
1/3 cup packed brown sugar
2 cups all-purpose flour
1 teaspoon baking powder
1/2 teaspoon baking soda
1 cup candied mixed fruit
1 tablespoon light sesame oil
1/4 teaspoon ground ginger
1/2 teaspoon ground cardamom
2 teaspoons ground cinnamon
1/4 teaspoon ground cloves
1/4 teaspoon ground allspice (optional)
1/4 teaspoon ground nutmeg (optional)
1 & 1/2 cups all-purpose flour

Spray the bottom and sides of a 10 x 15-inch glass pan with a non-stick spray. Preheat oven to 325 degrees.

In a 2-cup glass measuring cup, heat the honey and 1/3 cup sugar in a microwave for 1 minute. Pour this mixture into a medium mixing bowl. Sift together flour, baking powder, and baking soda. Add to the honey mixture. Stir well.

Add and mix in by hand the candied fruit, oil, and spices. Add 1 1/2 to 2 cups more flour. Knead dough to mix (dough will be stiff). Spread into pan. Bake for 20 minutes until inserted toothpick comes out clean.

Cut into squares. May be frosted with sugar glaze or eaten plain. Best if stored for 2 weeks.

Christmas Punch

Traditionally served on Christmas Eve
or Christmas Day

1 sliced pineapple
1 lb. sugar
1 bottle claret
1 bottle of red wine
1/2 bottle rum
juice of 4 lemons
juice of 4 oranges
1-pint water
grated rind of 1 lemon
grated rind of 1 orange
4 whole oranges cut in pieces
1 stick cinnamon, broken up
1 vanilla bean
1/2 cup maraschino cherries

Boil spices thoroughly with the water. Remove them and pour the water into large earthenware pot. Add lemon and orange and rind, as well as pineapple and sugar (fruit and sugar prepared in a separate dish). Then add wine and rum, cover and heat. Add champagne before serving.

This is strictly for the adults! The children in the family get another punch.

Christmas Punch for Children

1 qt. grape juice
2 qts. water
2 cups sugar
1/2 tsp. whole cloves
1 stick cinnamon
juice of 2 lemons
juice of 2 oranges
rind of 2 lemons
rind of 2 oranges

Boil sugar, water, lemon rind, and spices until flavored. Mix with the rest of the ingredients, boil five minutes, and serve hot in punch glasses.

Buche de Noel or Christmas Log

Traditionally served on Christmas Eve or Christmas Day

SPONGE CAKE:
4 eggs, separated and at room temperature
1 cup sugar
1/4 cup hot water
Grated rind of 1 lemon
1 teaspoon lemon juice
1/2 teaspoon vanilla
1 cup sifted flour
1 teaspoon baking powder

1/4 teaspoon salt
A few tablespoons rum (optional)
Confectioner's sugar

Preheat oven to 400 degrees. Grease a jelly-roll pan, 10 by 15 inches. Line the pan with waxed paper and grease the paper.

Beat the yolks until light and lemon colored. Gradually add the sugar, beating until very thick. Beat in the hot water, lemon rind, juice and vanilla.

Sift the flour with the baking powder and salt, and gradually beat into the egg mixture. Whip the egg whites until stiff but not dry. Fold gently but thoroughly into the batter.

Pour it into the jelly roll pan. Bake 12 to 15 minutes, or until the cake is lightly browned. As soon as the cake is done, sprinkle it with the rum if you wish.

Spread a clean, damp kitchen towel on the counter. Cover it with waxed paper. Sprinkle the paper with confectioners sugar. Invert the cake onto the waxed paper. Peel the paper off of the cake and trim the cake if too crusty. Roll up the cake along the long side with the towel and waxed paper. Let it cool to room temperature.

Mocha Cream Icing:

4 egg yolks

1.25cups sugar

1/3 cup water

2 teaspoons vanilla extract

2 teaspoons instant coffee

2 ounces unsweetened chocolate, melted and cooled

3 sticks (1.5cups) butter, at room temperature

Beat the yolks until light-colored and thick. Combine the sugar and water in a saucepan. Cook to the soft-ball stage: about 234 degrees on a candy thermometer. Beating constantly, add the eggs to the syrup. Continue beating until mixture is cool. Stir in the vanilla extract, coffee and chocolate. Gradually beat in the butter. Cool the icing in the refrigerator if it is too soft.

Assembling the Cake:

Unroll the cake. Spread it with half of the icing. Without the paper and the towel, roll it up as tightly as possible without damaging it.

Chill for several hours. Chill the icing as well. Trim the ends of the cake on the diagonal; reserve the scraps. Frost the cake with most of the remaining icing. Cut the scraps to resemble knot holes. Set them on the main log and ice them. Using the tines of a fork, make marks on the surface of the cake to look like bark.

Stollen
www.davidlebovitz.com/stollen/

2/3 cup dark raisins

2/3 cup golden raisins

1/2 cup dried cranberries or cherries

1/3 cup dark rum or orange juice

1 cup slivered or sliced almonds, lightly toasted

1/4 cup water

2 1/2 teaspoons powdered yeast

1/2 cup milk (whole or low-fat) at room temperature

3 1/2 cups all-purpose flour

1/2 cup rye flour,
  or use similar amount all-purpose flour

1/2 cup plus 3 tablespoons sugar

1 1/2 teaspoons ground dried ginger

1 teaspoon sea salt

1 teaspoon ground cinnamon

1 teaspoon ground cardamom

1 teaspoon freshly grated nutmeg

1 teaspoon grated lemon or orange zest,
  preferably unsprayed

3/4 teaspoon vanilla bean paste or extract

1 cup plus 3/4 cup unsalted butter, melted

1 tablespoon honey

1 large egg yolk

1/2 cup chopped candied ginger

1/2 cup diced candied citrus peel

1/2 cup powdered sugar or more, if necessary

1. Mix both kinds of raisins with cranberries or cherries with the dark rum or orange juice, then cover. In another bowl, mix the almonds with the water, and cover. Let both sit for at least an hour, or overnight.

2. Pour the milk in a medium bowl and sprinkle the yeast over it. Stir briefly, then stir in 1 cup (140 g) of the flour until smooth to make a starter. Cover, and let rest one hour.

3. In the bowl of a stand mixer, with the paddle attachment, or by hand, stir together the remaining 2 1/2 cups (350 g) flour, rye flour, 3 tablespoons (45 g) sugar, 1/2 teaspoon of dried ginger, salt, cinnamon, cardamom, nutmeg, citrus zest, and vanilla. Pour in 1 cup (8 ounces, 225 g) of the melted butter, honey, and the egg yolk, and mix on medium speed until mixture is moistened uniformly.

4. While mixing, add the yeast starter, one-third at a time, mixing until thoroughly incorporated. Once added, continue to beat for about four minutes until almost smooth: it should resemble cookie dough. Add the dried fruits (and any liquid), candied ginger, citrus peel, and almonds, and beat until they're well-distributed

5. Turn the dough out onto a lightly floured surface and knead a few times, then place back in the mixer bowl, cover, and let rest in a warm place for one hour.

6. Remove the dough from the bowl, knead the dough again, then return it to the bowl. Let rest for another hour.

7. Divide the dough into four pieces and shape each one into an oval, and place them evenly-spaced apart on an insulated baking sheet. (The original recipe says to stack two rimmed baking sheets on top of each other, so you can do that if you don't have one.)

8. Cover the loaves with a clean tea towel and let rest in a warm place for one hour.

9. Preheat the oven to 350F (180C). Remove the tea towel and bake the loaves for 45 minutes, or until they're deep golden brown. (Note: Recipe advises that when they're done, the internal temperature should read 190F, 88C if using an instant-read thermometer.)

10. While they loaves are baking, mix together the remaining 1/2 cup (100 g) sugar and 1 teaspoon dried ginger. When the breads come out of the oven, generously brush the remaining 3/4 cup (6 ounces, 170 g) melted butter over the hot loaves, letting the butter saturate the breads, repeating until all the butter is absorbed. (I was a daredevil and lifted the loaves, to saturate the bottoms. Which you can do if you feel nimble enough so you don't break the loaves.)

11. Rub the gingered sugar mixture over the top and

side of each loaf then let rest on the baking sheet until room temperature.

12. Sift powdered sugar over, under, and around the bread, rubbing it in with your hands. They wrap the loaves on the baking sheet in a large plastic bag and let them sit for two days. After two days, the loaves are ready to eat, or can be wrapped as gifts. You may wish to sift additional powdered sugar over the top in case they need another dusting.

Storage: Stollen can be stored for at least a week, if well-wrapped, at room temperature. Or frozen for at least one month.

Mulled Cider

Made on Christmas Day

2 quarts cider or apple juice
Peel of one orange or 2 teaspoons orange extract
1 to 2 sticks of cinnamon
1/2 tsp. allspice
1/2 tsp. cloves

Put all ingredients in a saucepan and bring to a boil. Lower the heat and simmer 5 to 10 minutes.

French Hot Chocolate

Made on Christmas Day

2 ounces dark chocolate per cup of whole milk

Heat the milk in a saucepan at a medium heat. Break the chocolate into small pieces and add to the milk. Stir until the chocolate is melted and serve.

Panettone (Italian Christmas Bread)

Ingredients:

MARINATED FRUIT:

1/3 cup golden raisins

1/3 cup chopped dried apricots

1/3 cup dried tart cherries

1/4 cup triple sec (orange-flavored liqueur)
  or orange juice

DOUGH:

1 package dry yeast (about 2 1/4 teaspoons)

1/4 teaspoon granulated sugar

1/4 cup warm water (100° to 110°)

3 3/4 cups all-purpose flour, divided

6 tablespoons butter or stick margarine, melted

1/4 cup whole milk

1/4 cup granulated sugar

1/2 teaspoon salt

1 large egg
1 large egg yolk
2 tablespoons pine nuts
Cooking spray
1 teaspoon butter, melted
2 teaspoons sugar

To prepare marinated fruit, combine first 4 ingredients in a small bowl; let stand 1 hour. Drain fruit in a sieve over a bowl, reserving fruit and 2 teaspoons liqueur separately. To prepare dough, dissolve yeast and 1/4 teaspoon granulated sugar in warm water in a small bowl; let stand 5 minutes. Lightly spoon flour into dry measuring cups; level with a knife. Combine 1/2 cup flour and next 6 ingredients (1/2 cup flour through egg yolk) in a large bowl; beat at medium speed of a mixer 1 minute or until smooth. Add yeast mixture and 1/2 cup flour; beat 1 minute. Stir in marinated fruit, 2 1/2 cups flour, and pine nuts. Turn dough out onto a lightly floured surface. Knead until smooth and elastic (about 8 minutes); add enough of remaining flour, 1 tablespoon at a time, to prevent dough from sticking to hands. Place dough in a large bowl coated with cooking spray, turning to coat top. Cover and let rise in a warm place (85°), free from drafts, about 1 1/2 hours. Dough will not double in size. (Press two fingers into dough. If indentation remains, the dough has risen enough.) Punch dough down; let rest 5 minutes. Divide in half, shaping each into a ball. Place balls into 2 (13-ounce) coffee cans coated with cooking spray. Cover and let rise 1 hour. Preheat oven to 375°. Uncover dough. Place coffee cans on bottom rack in oven and bake at 375° for 30 minutes or until browned and loaf sounds hollow when tapped. Remove bread from cans, and cool on a wire rack. Combine reserved 2 teaspoons liqueur and 1 teaspoon butter; brush over loaves. Sprinkle evenly with turbinado sugar.

From myrecipes.com

Eggnog

4 egg yolks
1/3 cup sugar, plus 1 tablespoon
1-pint whole milk
1 cup heavy cream
3 ounces bourbon
1 teaspoon freshly grated nutmeg
4 egg whites*

In the bowl of a stand mixer, beat the egg yolks until they lighten in color. Gradually add the 1/3 cup sugar and continue to beat until it is completely dissolved. Add the milk, cream, bourbon and nutmeg and stir to combine.

Place the egg whites in the bowl of a stand mixer and beat to soft peaks. With mixer still running gradually add 1 tablespoon of sugar and beat until stiff peaks form.

Whisk the egg whites into the mixture. Chill and serve.

Cook's Note: For cooked eggnog, follow the procedure below.

In the bowl of a stand mixer, beat the egg yolks until they lighten in color. Gradually add 1/3 cup sugar and continue to beat until it is completely dissolved. Set aside.

In a medium saucepan, over high heat, combine milk, heavy cream and nutmeg and bring just to a boil, stirring occasionally. Remove from the heat and gradually temper the hot mixture into the egg and sugar mixture. Then return everything to the pot and cook until mixture reaches 160 degrees F. Remove from the heat, stir in bourbon, pour into a medium mixing bowl, and set in the refrigerator to chill.

In a medium mixing bowl, beat the egg whites to soft peaks. With the mixer running gradually add 1 tablespoon of sugar and beat until stiff peaks form. Whisk the egg whites into the chilled mixture.

Recipe from foodnetwork.com

Homemade Tamales

TAMALE FILLING:

1 1/4 pounds pork loin

1 large onion, halved

1 clove garlic

4 dried California chile pods

2 cups water

1 1/2 teaspoons salt

TAMALE DOUGH:

2 cups masa harina

1 (10.5 ounce) can beef broth

1 teaspoon baking powder

1/2 teaspoon salt

2/3 cup lard

1 (8 ounce) package dried corn husks

1 cup sour cream

Place pork into a Dutch oven with onion and garlic and add water to cover. Bring to a boil, then reduce heat to low and simmer until the meat is cooked through, about 2 hours.

Use rubber gloves to remove stems and seeds from the chile pods. Place chiles in a saucepan with 2 cups of water. Simmer, uncovered, for 20 minutes, then remove from heat to cool. Transfer the chiles and water to a blender and blend until smooth. Strain the mixture, stir in salt, and set aside. Shred the cooked meat and mix in one cup of the chile sauce.

Soak the corn husks in a bowl of warm water. In a large bowl, beat the lard with a tablespoon of the broth until fluffy. Combine the masa harina, baking powder and salt; stir into the lard mixture, adding more broth as necessary to form a spongy dough.

Spread the dough out over the corn husks to 1/4 to 1/2-inch thickness. Place one tablespoon of the meat filling into the center. Fold the sides of the husks in toward the center and place in a steamer. Steam for 1 hour.

Remove tamales from husks and drizzle remaining chile sauce over. Top with sour cream. For a creamy sauce, mix sour cream into the chile sauce.

Recipe from allrecipes.com

Buñuelos (Mexican Fritters)

16 (1 fritter) Servings

FRITTERS

3 cups flour

1 tablespoon sugar

2 teaspoons baking powder

1/2 teaspoon salt

3/4 cup milk

1 egg

2 tablespoons lard, melted and cooled

2 teaspoons vanilla

Vegetable oil, for frying

CINNAMON SUGAR

1 cup sugar

1 tablespoon Cinnamon

ANISE SYRUP (OPTIONAL)

2 cups water

8 ounces piloncillo, (panela), coarsely chopped

1 teaspoon grated lime peel

1 teaspoon grated orange peel

2 Cinnamon Sticks

2 teaspoons Anise Seed

For the Fritters, mix flour, sugar, baking powder and salt in medium bowl. Set aside. Mix milk, egg, lard and vanilla in large bowl until well blended. Gradually add flour mixture, stirring constantly to form a slightly sticky dough. Turn dough out onto lightly floured surface. Incorporate additional flour, a tablespoon flour at a time, until dough is no longer sticky. Divide dough into 16 equal pieces. Shape each into a ball. Place in bowl. Cover with plastic wrap. Let dough rest 30 minutes.

Meanwhile, for the Cinnamon Sugar, mix sugar and cinnamon in medium bowl. Set aside. For the Anise Syrup, mix water, piloncillo, lime peel, orange peel, cinnamon sticks and anise seed in heavy-bottomed 3-quart saucepan. Cook on medium heat 5 minutes, stirring to dissolve piloncillo. Bring to boil on medium-high heat. Boil 20 minutes or until syrup thinly coats a spoon. Strain and set aside at room temperature. (Anise Syrup can be made 3 to 4 days ahead. Cover and refrigerate. Rewarm before using.)

Roll each ball of dough into a 6-inch round on lightly floured surface. Stack dough rounds between wax paper or plastic wrap. Let stand 10 minutes. Pour vegetable oil into heavy large skillet or saucepan to depth of 1 inch (about 2 cups oil). Heat oil on medium-high heat to 365°F to 370°F on deep-fry thermometer. Fry dough rounds, 1 at a time, for 2 minutes or until golden and puffed, turning once using tongs. Drain on paper towels. Sprinkle each fritter with 1 tablespoon cinnamon sugar mixture. Serve with warm Anise Syrup, if desired.

Recipe from McCormick.com

Ponche (Mexican Christmas Punch)
PONCHE NAVIDEÑO (MEXICAN
CHRISTMAS FRUIT PUNCH)

4 quarts water

2 cinnamon sticks

8 whole cloves

5 long tamarind pods, husk removed, and seeded
  or boil the entire pod to make removing easier

½ pound tejocotes or crab apples, left whole

6 large guavas, peeled and cut into large bite-size chunks

2 red apples (of your choice), peeled, cored, and cut into
  small bite-size chunks

1 pear (of your choice), peeled, cored, and cut into small
  bite-size chunks

2 (4-inch) sugarcane sticks, peeled and cut into
  small chunks

1 cup pitted prunes

1/2 cup dark raisins

1 orange, sliced

1 cone piloncillo, chopped or 1 cup dark brown sugar

1-ounce brandy or tequila per cup (optional)

In a large pot, over high heat, boil water, cinnamon
sticks, cloves, tamarind, and tejocotes. After it starts to
boil, lower the heat and simmer for about 10 minutes
until the tejocotes are soft.

Remove the tejocotes from the heat, peel, remove hard

ends, cut in half, and deseed. Return them to the pot.

Add guavas, apples, pears, sugar cane, prunes, orange slices, and piloncillo.

Simmer for at least 30 minutes, stirring gently. Discard cinnamon sticks and cloves.

Ladle into cups, making sure each cup gets some chunks of fruit.

Add brandy or tequila to each cup (optional).

Recipe from muybuenocooking.com

Kerala Fruit Cake from India

1 cup plain flour

½ cup chopped cashew nuts

¼ cup black raisins

½ cup mixed dry fruits (dates, cherries, orange peels, etc.)

½ cup white sugar (for sugar syrup)

¾ cup white sugar (for cake batter)

⅔ cup unsalted butter, at room temperature

3 eggs

½ tsp cinnamon powder

¼ tsp clove powder (see notes)

1 tsp of baking powder

1 tsp vanilla extract

A pinch of salt

1. In a pan on medium heat, melt ½ cup sugar slowly.

2. It will first melt and then turn into a dark brown goop. Keep stirring and let it turn a deep dark caramel color. Don't let it burn.

3. Turn off heat and add about ¼ cup water. The sugar will harden.

4. Turn the heat back on and slowly heat the mixture until the sugar crystals dissolve.

5. This will take around 10 mins.

6. Let this cool and set aside.

7. Preheat oven to 350F / 180C.

8. Add 3 tbsp flour to the dry fruits and nuts and dredge completely to coat it. This is so that they don't sink to the bottom of the batter while baking. Set aside.

9. Mix the remaining flour and baking powder, spices, and salt until well combined.

10. Beat the butter and ¾ cup sugar until fluffy - about 10 mins by hand, 3-4 mins with an electric beater. Add vanilla and mix until combined. Next, add 1 egg and beat. Then add a bit of the flour mixture and fold. Likewise, alternate between the eggs and flour mixture until they are used up.

11. Add the cooled caramel and dredged fruits and

gently fold in. Pour batter into a greased cake pan and smooth the top.

12. Bake for 50-55 minutes until the top turns a dark brown and when a skewer inserted into the cake comes out with dry crumbs.

13. Start checking from 45 mins to see if the cake is done.

14. The top will look like it's overdone but don't worry, make sure the inside is also completely cooked.

15. Dust with icing sugar when the cake is completely cooled Recipe from cookingandme.com

Indian Rice Pudding (Kheer)

¼ cup Long grain rice or Basmati rice

2 ½ cups Milk

¼ cup Sugar

¼ teaspoon Green cardamom seeds powder

few strands Saffron

½ tablespoon Almonds

½ tablespoon Cashew nuts

½ tablespoon Raisins

1. Wash the rice under running cold water till water runs clear.

2. Soak them in enough water for 20-30 minutes.

3. While rice is soaking, chop the nuts and keep it aside.

4. After soaking time, discard the water.

MAKING RICE KHEER RECIPE:

1. Take milk in a heavy bottom pan. Turn the heat on medium.

2. Let the milk come to a boil.

3. Once it starts boiling, add rice.

4. Stir well and let it simmer on low-medium heat 20-25 minutes. Or till the rice is tender and cooked. Do stir every five minutes and make sure that rice or milk is not sticking to the pan.

5. Check by pinching the rice grain, it will mash very easily. When you take a spoonful of it and pour it back, rice and milk stay separate.

6. Now add sugar and cardamom powder. Stir it well.

7. Also add saffron strands and chopped cashews, almonds and raisins.

8. Mix well. let it simmer for 6-7 minutes. It should be thick now.

9. How to check right consistency: take ladleful of kheer and pour it back. rice and milk should fall together in the same flow. They should not be separated like earlier.

Recipe from cookingandme.com

Making Anglicanism Accessible

Whether you're an Anglican leader or just "Angli-curious," Anglican Pastor has the resources you need to follow Jesus in the Anglican way. We write with clarity and charity about the Anglican tradition, in order to enrich churches on the ground today.

If you'd like to take advantage of what we have to offer, please subscribe to our email list at anglicanpastor.com/subscribe.

In exchange for your email address, we will give you the latest edition of our *Daily Office Booklet*, an easy-to-use resource for doing Morning and Evening Prayer on your own or with a group!

Get your FREE Daily Office Booklet at
anglicanpastor.com/subscribe

If you'd like to get in touch
with Ashley Wallace,
you can visit her website at
www.seasonsofthechurch.com

Made in the USA
Coppell, TX
28 November 2019

11964097R00065